P9-DDA-198

For
Gwen with
thanks for putting
up with me!
♡. Love Lawrie

SISTERS

Thoughts on that Special Relationship

Compiled by
Lois L. Kaufman

Design by
Deborah Michel

PETER PAUPER PRESS, INC.
WHITE PLAINS, NEW YORK

For My Sisters,
Doris and Carol

Photo color tints by Marc Jaffe

Copyright © 1993
Peter Pauper Press, Inc.
202 Mamaroneck Avenue
White Plains, NY 10601
All rights reserved
ISBN 0-88088-501-7
Printed in Singapore
7 6

Contents

Introduction

The quotations that follow deal with a very special relationship, either by birth or by affinity. Whether sisters are geographically close or distant, an emotional tie always connects them, showing itself sometimes in affection, and sometimes in conflict or a Tug of War.

Sisterhood among women in general has never been so significant as at present. It is a growing movement, and promises to change the course of our history.

Sisters can be pets, or pet peeves. A sister can be a friend, and a friend can be a sister. However we may regard them, either as our mirror images or our opposites, sisters are an important part of our lives.

L. L. K.

Peas In A Pod

$\mathcal{I}$ have got a new-born sister;
I was nigh the first that kissed her.
When the nursing-woman brought her
To papa, his infant daughter,
How papa's dear eyes did glisten!—
She will shortly be to christen;
And papa has made the offer,
I shall have the naming of her.

Now I wonder what would please her,—
Charlotte, Julia, or Louisa?
Ann and Mary, they're too common;
Joan's too formal for a woman;
Jane's a prettier name beside;
But we had a Jane that died.
They would say, if 't was Rebecca,
That she was a little Quaker.
Edith's pretty, but that looks
Better in old English books;
Ellen's left off long ago;
Blanche is out of fashion now.
None that I have named as yet
Are so good as Margaret.
Emily is neat and fine;
What do you think of Caroline?
How I'm puzzled and perplexed
What to choose or think of next!
I am in a little fever
Lest the name that I should give her
Should disgrace her or defame her;—
I will leave papa to name her.

MARY LAMB,
Choosing a Name

$\mathscr{A}$ ministering angel shall my sister be.

WILLIAM SHAKESPEARE,
Hamlet

$\mathscr{W}$e acquire friends and we make enemies, but our sisters come with the territory.

EVELYN LOEB

$\mathscr{A}$ll three sisters had the same high-bridged noses; Roman noses, my mother said. I pored over these pictures, intrigued by the idea of the triplicate, identical noses. I did not have a sister myself, then, and the mystique of sisterhood was potent for me.

MARGARET ATWOOD

$\mathscr{S}$isters are our peers, the voice of our times.

ELIZABETH FISHEL

$\mathscr{S}$isters stand between one and life's cruel circumstances.

NANCY MILFORD

$\mathscr{S}$isterly love is, of all sentiments, the most abstract. Nature does not grant it any functions.

UGO BETTI,
The Gambler

8

$\mathcal{S}$ixty-six years ago tonight I was hardly me. I was just a pink bundle snuggled in a blanket close to Mother. . . . The night before had been a disturbed one for everybody. Everything was quieted down tonight. The two-year-old Alice was deposed from her baby throne. The bigger girls were sprouting motherisms, all-over delighted with the new toy.

EMILY CARR

$\mathcal{S}$chool parted us; we never found again
That childish world where our two spirits
　　mingled
Like scents from varying roses that
　　remain
One sweetness, nor can evermore be
　　singled.

Yet the twin habit of that early time
Lingered for long about the heart and
　　tongue:
We had been natives of one happy clime,
And its dear accent to our utterance
　　clung.

Till the dire years whose awful name is
　　Change
Had grasped our souls still yearning in
　　divorce,
And pitiless shaped them in two forms
　　that range
Two elements which sever their life's
　　course.

But were another childhood-world
　　　　my share,
I would be born a little sister there.

GEORGE ELIOT,
School Parted Us

But however you might rebel, there was no shedding them. They were your responsibility and there was no one to relieve you of them. They called you Sis. All your life people called you Sis, because that was what you were, or what you became—big sister, helpful sister, the one upon whom everyone depended, the one they all came to for everything from help with homework to a sliver under the fingernail.

WALLACE STEGNER

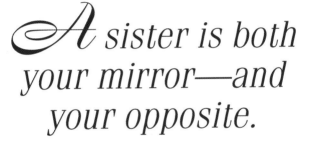

A sister is both your mirror—and your opposite.

ELIZABETH FISHEL

I was always putting myself in my sister's place, adopting her credulousness, and even her memories, I saw, could be made mine. It was Isobel I imagined as the eternal heroine—never myself. I substituted her feelings for my own, and her face for any face described. Whatever the author's intentions, the heroine was my sister.

MAVIS GALLANT

11

$\mathcal{B}$abe was always the glamor girl and I was always the crumbum except when I was away from her. Babe was a perfectionist. Compared to her I always felt insecure.

BETSY WHITNEY,
about her sister, Babe Paley

$\mathcal{I}$ might have seen more of America when I was a child if I hadn't had to spend so much of my time protecting my half of the back seat from incursions by sister, Sukey.

CALVIN TRILLIN

$\mathcal{I}$ was always wanting more from Susan. More time. More attention. More love. She always wanted me to bug off. . . . Despite my underlying resentment, my sister's presence always mattered. How happy I was to see her waiting outside school for me the day I got my first report card. How crushed I was the night my friend Ellen and I put on *The Pajama Game* for our families and Susan was out with her friends. . . . We are sisters. We will always be sisters. Our differences may never go away, but neither, for me, will our song.

NANCY KELTON

$\mathcal{M}$y sister Doris, though two years younger than I, had enough gumption for a dozen people. . . . When she was only seven she could carry a piece of short-weighted cheese back to the A & P, threaten the manager with legal action, and come back triumphantly with the full quarter-pound we'd paid for and a few ounces extra thrown in for forgiveness. Doris could have made something of herself if she hadn't been a girl. Because of this defect, however, the best she could hope for was a career as a nurse or schoolteacher, the only work that capable females were considered up to in those days.

RUSSELL BAKER,
Growing Up

$\mathcal{T}$he Cushing sisters made every man they married far better men than they really were.

TEX MCCRARY

13

How could I be jealous of her? Everything she has she shares with me. I had a life-threatening illness just about the time she started to make it in TV. I had just come out of a coma when she came to the hospital and leaned over my bed and whispered, "Little Mich, little Mich, don't you worry about anything. Wherever I go, I'll take care of you." And she has.

MICHIE NADER,
sister of Kathie Lee Gifford

Once my big sister found and read something I wrote at the midnight of a new year. I was sorry about the old year, I had seemed to have failed so, and I had hopes for the new. But when she hurled my written thoughts at me I was angry and humbled and hurt and I burst smarting into the New Year and broke all my resolutions and didn't care. I burnt the diary and buried the thoughts and felt the world was a mean, sneaking place.

EMILY CARR

It was [her sister] Sheyna who gave meaning to Golda's consciousness of being different. She made Golda proud to be a Jew. Sheyna, who Golda says was the greatest influence on her life apart from her husband, was a Zionist, and Zionists believed that Jews not only had a right to exist, but also had an historic mission as well—to return to Zion and establish a land of their own. And Golda accepted this mission.

JULIE NIXON EISENHOWER,
on Golda Meir

It is true that I was born in Iowa, but I can't speak for my twin sister.

ABIGAIL VAN BUREN,
Dear Abby

No matter what her mood, Charles was unfailingly supportive of his sister, calm and cheerful, even though occasionally she openly expressed her impatience with him as well. There were times when he would stop to talk with people and thus delay our departure for a few moments and Anne, by her comments, would let him know that it irritated her to have to wait for him. It was a typical sisterly reaction—and would have gone unnoticed with any other brother and sister. But this was the Prince of Wales, the future King, and this was his sister. And the whole of Washington seemed fascinated by their every expression, word and gesture.

JULIE NIXON EISENHOWER

Children of the same mother do not always agree.

NIGERIAN PROVERB

The older daughter is married off by her parents, the younger daughter by her sister.

RUSSIAN PROVERB

Her name was Margaret Lucas, youngest sister to the Lord Lucas of Colchester, a Noble Familie: for all the brothers were valiant and all the sisters virtuous.

EPITAPH ON MARGARET, DUCHESS OF NEWCASTLE,
Westminster Abbey

When my sister made a courageous decision to go to law school at the age of fifty, leaving my mother in a house that not only had many loving teenage grandchildren in it but a kindly older woman as a paid companion besides, my mother reduced her to frequent tears by insisting that this was a family with no love in it, no home-cooked food in the refrigerator; not a real family at all.

GLORIA STEINEM

I shall never consent to have our sex considered in an inferior point of light.

ABIGAIL ADAMS,
to her sister Elizabeth

$\mathcal{T}$he love that grew with us from our cradles never knew diminution from time or distance. Other ties were formed, but they did not supersede or weaken this. Death tore away all that was mortal and perishable, but this tie he could not sunder.

CHARLOTTE ELIZABETH TONNA

17

But I am truest speaker: you call'd me
  brother
When I was but your sister.

WILLIAM SHAKESPEARE,
Cymbeline

It's quite as real an experience as having a baby
or anything else, being moved as you have
succeeded in moving me.

VIRGINIA WOOLF,
about her sister Vanessa Bell's writing

Mummy certainly feels that Margot loves her
much more than I do, but she thinks that this just
goes in phases! Margot has grown so sweet; she
seems quite different from what she used to be, isn't
nearly so catty these days and is becoming a real
friend. Nor does she any longer regard me as a little
kid who counts for nothing.

ANNE FRANK

She was never dressed as a boy. She was
beautiful. She made a beautiful picture, but she
didn't like vaudeville. She didn't know why she
should bother to learn to sing and dance, and get
tired, if she didn't have to. . . . I wish my sister
hadn't died at an early age. That she could have had
the exquisite joy of growing old.

JUNE HAVOC,
on her sister, Gypsy Rose Lee

*Y*ou can't think how I depend upon you, and when you're not there the colour goes out of my life, as water from a sponge; and I merely exist, dry and dusty. This is the exact truth: but not a very beautiful illustration of my complete adoration of you; and longing to sit, even saying nothing, and look at you.

VIRGINIA WOOLF,
to Vanessa Bell

*M*y sister! With that thrilling word
  Let thoughts unnumbered wildly spring!
What echoes in my heart are stirred,
  While thus I touch the trembling string.

MARGARET DAVIDSON

$\mathscr{I}$ cannot deny that, now I am without your company I feel not only that I am deprived of a very dear sister, but that I have lost half of myself.

BEATRICE D'ESTE,
letter to her sister, Isabella d'Este

$\mathscr{S}$isters may
share the same
mother and father
but appear to come
from different
families.

$\mathscr{T}$he intensity between brother and sister is likely to be less than that between two sisters because men and women occupy different spheres in relation to child rearing.

KAREN GAIL LEWIS

$\mathscr{A}$n older sister helps one remain half child, half woman.

For there is no friend like a sister,
In calm or stormy weather,
To cheer one on the tedious way,
To fetch one if one goes astray,
To lift one if one totters down,
To strengthen whilst one stands.

CHRISTINA ROSSETTI,
Goblin Market

I sought my soul,
  But my soul I could not see.
I sought my God,
  But my God eluded me.
I sought my sisters,
  And I found all three.

ANONYMOUS

[She is] a bowl of golden water which brims but
never overflows.

VIRGINIA WOOLF,
about her sister, Vanessa Bell

Big sisters are the crab grass in the lawn of
life.

CHARLES M. SCHULZ,
Peanuts

$\mathcal{T}$here are women who don't have a good relationship with their sisters but who wish it were otherwise. Having kids can be a turning point. Their relationship can become revitalized and reinvigorated.

MICHAEL KAHN

$\mathcal{T}$wo highlights of my youth revolve around Sandy. The first: she got married when I was six, which is *the* memory of my childhood because one of my aunts fell through the floor at her wedding. [The other is] when my mother asked Sandy to pick me up at the June Taylor School of the Dance and take me to Howard Johnson and Radio City Music Hall, as we did every Saturday. So Sandra, married and divorced by now and home on vacation from London, took me instead to the House of Chad where we ate lobster and spare ribs and all these things I thought were going to make me drop dead, and then she took me to this movie called *Expresso Bongo*.

WENDY WASSERSTEIN

$\mathcal{I}$ don't want to be in the least like Margot. She is much too soft and passive for my liking and allows everyone to talk her around, and gives in about everything. I want to be a stronger character!

ANNE FRANK

$\mathcal{G}$one are those three, those sisters rare
With wonder-lips and eyes ashine.
One was wise, and one was fair,
And one was mine.

ARTHUR DAVISON FICKE,
The Three Sisters

$\mathcal{F}$or when three sisters love each other with
such sincere affection, the one does not experience
sorrow, pain, or affliction of any kind, but the
others' heart wishes to relieve, and vibrates in
tenderness. Like a well-organized musical
instrument.

ELIZABETH SHAW,
sister of Abigail Adams and Mary Cranch

Here lies Fred,
Who was alive and is dead;
Had it been his father,
I had much rather;
Had it been his brother,
Still better than the other;
Had it been his sister,
No one would have missed her;
Had it been the whole generation,
All the better for the nation;
But since 'tis only Fred,
That was alive and is dead,
Why, there's no more to be said.

EPITAPh ON FREDERICK,
PRINCE OF WALES, *1751*

Two sisters from the same old home
  Now meet no more in life;
For one the smiles of fortune fair,
  For one its frown and strife.
Their paths are parted far and wide,
  Since they were young and gay,
And so the simple story runs,
  Of life from day to day.

CHARLES A. WILSON,
Two Sisters from the Same Old Home

Call
Me
Sister

$\mathcal{H}$elp one another is part of the religion of our sisterhood, Fan.

LOUISA MAY ALCOTT,
An Old-Fashioned Girl

$\mathcal{W}$e are together, my child and I. Mother and child, yes, but *sisters* really, against whatever denies us all that we are.

ALICE WALKER

$\mathcal{I}$ am not afraid to trust my sisters—not I.

ANGELA GRIMKE

We older women who know we aren't heroines can offer our younger sisters, at the very least, an honest report of what we have learned and how we have grown.

ELIZABETH JANEWAY

Sitting in an ethnic hall in Detroit, at a local celebration of *Ms.* magazine's tenth birthday, and being tapped on the shoulder by a small, gray-haired woman with gnarled, hardworking hands and a starched cotton housedress that is clearly her best. "I just want you to know," she says softly, "that you are the inside of me." All reward came together in one moment. Remembering now that woman's touch and words, I still feel the tears behind my eyes.

GLORIA STEINEM

All women have a sacred obligation to each other irrespective of class or conditions of work.

VIDA GOLDSTEIN

We express thanks for the common bond which underlies all the uncommonness—the bond which enables us to come together at this special 40th reunion, after years of separation, with a sense of closeness that is both rare and precious.

BEA YAMASAKI,
from a grace given at a
Mt. Holyoke College reunion dinner

27

*T*he reason that there are so few women comics is that so few women can bear being laughed at.

ANNA RUSSELL

*W*omen who set a low value on themselves make life hard for all women.

NELLIE McCLUNG

I like to help women help themselves, as that is, in my opinion, the best way to settle the woman question. Whatever we can do and do well we have a right to, and I don't think any one will deny us.

LOUISA MAY ALCOTT

I am thoroughly against women becoming soldiers. It goes against everything we stand for as sisters, as nurturers. Women are the civilizers. To join the draft is to join the killers.

DR. HELEN CALDICOTT

*W*omen never have young minds. They are born three thousand years old.

SHELAGH DELANEY

. . . *t*he righteous grapevine of womenfolk.

JOHNNETTA B. COLE

$\mathcal{B}$ut the women we really are can only live if we break open the secret. How many daughters, mothers, sisters, godmothers, and grandmothers, aunts, cousins and best friends have lived and died unknown? Each woman's forced silence was a denial of her existence, as if she never loved another woman, never rejoiced in their union, or cried for her, or waited for her to come home.

JUANITA RAMOS

$\mathcal{O}$ur sex are seldom kind to the woman that is so prosperous, their pity is confined to those that are forsaken—to be forsaken and ugly are the greatest distresses a woman can have.

ELIZABETH INCHBALD

$\mathcal{A}$t my age I care to my roots about the quality of women, and I care because I know how important her quality is. The hurt that women have borne so long may have immeasurable meaning. We women are the meeting place of the highest and the lowest, and of minutia and riches; it is for us to see, and understand, and have pride in representing ourselves truly. Perhaps we must say to man . . . "The time may have come for us to forge our own identity, dangerous as that will be."

FLORIDA SCOTT-MAXWELL

$\mathcal{T}$he bond between women is a circle—we are together within it.

JUDY GRAHN

I've always believed that one woman's success can only help another woman's success.

GLORIA VANDERBILT

*A*nd for my sisters a great love and pity fills my heart . . . I love you, I love you. Bravely you jog along with the rope of class distinction drawing closer, closer, tighter, tighter around you . . . I am only one of yourselves, I am only an unnecessary, little, bush commoner, I am only a—woman.

MILES FRANKLIN

*I*t is only the women whose eyes have been washed clear with tears who get the broad vision that makes them little sisters to all the world.

DOROTHY DIX

I spend a lot of time talking to women and to women's groups trying to convince them that the experiences they've had in life are as valid as any experiences men have had. I think that needs to be said again and again.

CAROLINE HOGG

*W*e need to know the history of our sisters, both for inspiration and for accumulating a full arsenal of ideas, and adopt what translates into the present.

GLORIA STEINEM

*O*ne is not born a woman—one becomes one.
SIMONE DE BEAUVOIR

*W*hether women are better than men I cannot say—but I can say they are certainly no worse.

GOLDA MEIR

*W*hat did the Colonel's Lady think?
  Nobody ever knew.
Somebody asked the Sergeant's Wife,
  An' she told 'em true!
When you get to a man in the case,
  They're like as a row of pins—
For the Colonel's Lady an' Judy O'Grady
  Are sisters under their skins!

RUDYARD KIPLING,
The Ladies

I was a woman before I was an abolitionist. I must speak for the women.

LUCY STONE

Tug

of

War

$\mathcal{A}$ sibling is any other kid your mother and father have around the house. You will not like him (her). He (she) will not like you. Make friends with him (her) anyhow. It evens up the odds with your parents.

ROBERT PAUL SMITH

$\mathcal{N}$ever praise a sister to a sister, in the hope of your compliments reaching the proper ears.

RUDYARD KIPLING

$\mathcal{T}$rue sibling relationships have a varied lot of ingredients, but sympathy is rarely one of them.

JUDITH MARTIN,
Miss Manners

$\mathcal{D}$umb. Dumb. Tiny drum beats. Dumb. Dumb. Her sister's favorite word. She called her dumb more than she called her Jane.

ANN MCGOVERN

$\mathcal{T}$here is only one person an English girl hates more than she hates her elder sister; and that is her mother.

GEORGE BERNARD SHAW

$\mathcal{J}$ealousy and love are sisters.

RUSSIAN PROVERB

$\mathcal{T}$he young ladies entered the drawing-room in the full fervour of sisterly animosity.

R. S. SURTEES,
Mr. Sponge's Sporting Tour

$\mathcal{S}$ibling rivalry is not an evil born of parental failure. It is a fact of life.

SEYMOUR V. REIT

For the lips of a strange woman drop as an honeycomb, and her mouth is smoother than oil: But her end is bitter as wormwood, sharp as a two-edged sword.

PROVERBS 5:3-4

. . . *As* nobody can do more mischief to a woman than a woman, so perhaps might one reverse the maxim and say nobody can do more good.

ELIZABETH HOLLAND

If you want to know how old a woman is, ask her sister-in-law.

E. W. HOWE

Jealousy does more harm than witchcraft.

GERMAN PROVERB

It is very hard that a pretty woman is never to be told she is so by any one of her own sex without that person's being suspected to be either her determined Enemy, or her professed Toadeater.

JANE AUSTEN

There is more self-love than love in jealousy.

LA ROCHEFOUCAULD

My
Sister,
My
Friend

*S*he is such a good friend that she would throw all her acquaintances into the water for the pleasure of fishing them out.

TALLEYRAND,
about Mme. de Staël

*I*n thee my soul shall own combined
The sister and the friend.

CATHERINE KILLIGREW

$\mathcal{I}$ntimacies between women often go backwards, beginning in revelations and ending in small talk without loss of esteem.

ELIZABETH BOWEN

$\mathcal{W}$e shelter children for a time; we live side by side with men; and that is all. We owe them nothing, and are owed nothing. I think we owe our friends more, especially our female friends.

FAY WELDON

$\mathcal{T}$hough not your kin, a friend is your best relation.

HINDU PROVERB

$\mathcal{I}$ found real love in girlfriends . . . I've always found girls I've loved and who've made me laugh. It's just nice—a really good friendship.

TINA TURNER

$\mathcal{M}$any kinds of fruit grow upon the tree of life, but none so sweet as friendship; as with the orange tree its blossoms and fruit appear at the same time, full of refreshment for sense and for soul.

LUCY LARCOM

$\mathcal{W}$ent through our friendships like epsom salts, draining us, no apologies, no regrets.

ROSA GUY

Two may talk together under the same roof for many years, yet never really meet; and two others at first speech are old friends.

MARY CATHERWOOD

We have been friends together
In sunshine and shade.

CAROLINE NORTON

My friendship [with Vita Sackville-West] is over. Not with a quarrel, not with a bang, but as a ripe fruit falls.

VIRGINIA WOOLF

But every road is rough to me that has no friend to cheer it.

ELIZABETH SHANE

When the sun shines on you, you see your friends. Friends are the thermometers by which one may judge the temperature of our fortunes.

COUNTESS OF BLESSINGTON

After an acquaintance of ten minutes many women will exchange confidences that a man would not reveal to a lifelong friend.

PAGE SMITH

ℰach friend represents a world in us, a world
possibly not born until they arrive, and it is only by
this meeting that a new world is born.

ANAIS NIN

*W*hen you come to the end of a perfect
  day,
And you sit alone with your thought,
While the chimes ring out with a carol gay
For the joy that the day has brought,
Do you think what the end of a perfect
  day
Can mean to a tired heart,
When the sun goes down with a flaming
  ray,
And the dear friends have to part?

Well, this is the end of a perfect day,
Near the end of a journey, too;
But it leaves a thought that is big and
  strong,
With a wish that is kind and true.
For mem'ry has painted this perfect day
With colors that never fade,
And we find, at the end of a perfect day,
The soul of a friend we've made.

CARRIE JACOBS BOND,
A Perfect Day

*M*y only sketch, profile, of Heaven is a large
blue sky, and larger than the biggest I have seen in
June—and in it are my friends—every one of them.

EMILY DICKINSON

*O*h, the comfort—the inexpressible
   comfort of feeling safe with a person,
Having neither to weigh thoughts,
Nor measure words—but pouring them
All right out—just as they are—
Chaff and grain together—
Certain that a faithful hand will
Take and sift them—
Keep what is worth keeping—
And with the breath of kindness
Blow the rest away.

DINAH MARIA MULOCK CRAIK,
Nor Measure Words

The only thing to do is to hug one's friends tight and do one's job.

EDITH WHARTON

The heart may think it knows better: the senses know that absence blots people out. We have really no absent friends.

ELIZABETH BOWEN

In their friendship they were like two of a litter than can never play together without leaving traces of tooth and claw, wounding each other in the most sensitive places.

COLETTE

As we sail through life towards death,
Bound unto the same port—heaven,—
Friend, what years could us divide?

DINAH MARIA MULOCK CRAIK,
A Christmas Blessing

Acknowledgments

Cover photograph and photographs on pages 17, 19, and 33 are reproduced, with permission, from the collection of Barbara Kohn.

Photograph on page 4 is reproduced, with permission, from the collection of Sara A. Linder.

Photographs on pages 12, 23, 26, 40, and 45 are reproduced, with permission, from the collection of Iris Brock.

Photographs on pages 29 and 37 are reproduced, with permission, from the collection of the Fetzer family.

Photograph on page 30 is reproduced, with permission, from the collection of Evelyn Loeb.

Photograph on page 43 is reproduced, with permission, from the collection of Paulette Pomeranz.